Succeed on the Standardized Test

This Book Includes:

- 2 Performance Based Assessments (PBA)
- 2 End-Of-Year (EOY) Assessments
- Detailed Answer explanations for every question
- Type I questions - Concepts, Skills and Procedures
  Type II questions - Expressing Mathematical Reasoning
  Type III questions - Modeling and/or Applications
- Strategies for building speed and accuracy
- Content aligned with the new Common Core State Standards

Plus access to Online Workbooks which include:

- Hundreds of practice questions
- Self-paced learning and personalized score reports
- Instant feedback after completion of the workbook

Complement Classroom Learning All Year

Using the Lumos Study Program, parents and teachers can reinforce the classroom learning experience for children. It creates a collaborative learning platform for students, teachers and parents.

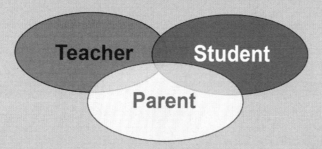

Used in Schools and Public Libraries To Improve Student Achievement

Lumos Learning

Common Core Assessments and Online Workbooks: Grade 3 Mathematics, PARCC Edition

Contributing Editor   - Marcia Weishaar
Contributing Editor   - George Smith
Contributing Editor   - Gregory Applegate
Contributing Editor   - LaSina McLain-Jackson
Curriculum Director   - Marisa Adams
Executive Producer   - Mukunda Krishnaswamy
Illustrator & Designer - Mirona Jova

ISBN-10: 1940484189

ISBN-13: 978-1-940484-18-1

Printed in the United States of America

For permissions and additional information contact us

Lumos Information Services, LLC
PO Box 1575, Piscataway, NJ 08855-1575
http://www.LumosLearning.com

Email: support@lumoslearning.com
Tel: (732) 384-0146
Fax: (866) 283-6471

Lumos Learning

Table of Contents

Introduction

The Common Core State Standards Initiative (CCSS) was created from the need to have more robust and rigorous guidelines, which could be standardized from state to state. These guidelines create a learning environment where students will be able to graduate high school with all skills necessary to be active and successful members of society, whether they take a role in the workforce or in some sort of post-secondary education.

Once the CCSS were fully developed and implemented, it became necessary to devise a way to ensure they were assessed appropriately. To this end, states adopting the CCSS have joined one of two consortia, either PARCC or Smarter Balanced.

What is PARCC?

The Partnership for Assessment of Readiness for College and Careers (PARCC) is one of the two state consortiums responsible for developing assessments aligned to the new, more rigorous Common Core State Standards. A combination of educational leaders from PARCC Governing and Participating states, along with test developers, have worked together to create the new computer based English Language Arts and Math Assessments.

PARCC has spent the better part of two years developing their new assessments, and in many ways, they will be unlike anything many students have ever seen. The tests will be conducted online, requiring students to complete tasks to assess a deeper understanding of the CCSS. Additionally, instead of one final test at the end of the year, PARCC understands that the best way to measure student success is to assess them multiple times a year. So, students in PARCC states will take a mid-year assessment called a Performance Based Assessment (PBA) and an End-of-Year Assessment (EOY).

How Can the Lumos Study Program Prepare Students for PARCC Tests?

Beginning in the fall of 2014, student mastery of Common Core State Standards will be assessed using standardized testing methods. At Lumos Learning, we believe that year-long learning and adequate practice before the actual test are the keys to success on these standardized tests. We have designed the Lumos study program to help students get plenty of realistic practice before the test and to promote year long collaborative learning.

This is a Lumos **tedBook**™. It connects you to Online Workbooks and additional resources using a number of devices including Android phones, iPhones, tablets and personal computers. The Lumos StepUp Online Workbooks are designed to promote year-long learning. It is a simple program students can securely access using a computer or device with internet access. It consists of hundreds of grade appropriate questions, aligned to the new Common Core State Standards. Students will get instant feedback and can review their answers anytime. Each student's answers and progress can be reviewed by parents and educators to reinforce the learning experience.

     LumosLearning.com

How to use this book effectively

The Lumos Program is a flexible learning tool. It can be adapted to suit a student's skill level and the time available to practice before standardized tests. Here are some tips to help you use this book and the online workbooks effectively:

Students

- Take one Performance Based Assessment (PBA).
- Use the "Related Lumos StepUp™ Online Workbook" in the Answer Key section to identify the topic that is related to each question.
- Use the Online workbooks to practice your areas of difficulty and complement classroom learning.
- Download the Lumos StepUp™ app using the instructions provided in Lumos StepUp™ Mobile App FAQ to have anywhere access to online resources.
- Have open-ended questions evaluated by a teacher or parent, keeping in mind the scoring rubrics.
- Take the second PBA as you get close to the test date.
- Complete the test in a quiet place, following the test guidelines. Practice tests provide you an opportunity to improve your test-taking skills and to review topics included in the PARCC test.
- As the end of the year becomes closer, take one EOY and follow the above guidelines before taking the second.

Parents

- Familiarize yourself with the PARCC test format and expectations.
- Help your child use Lumos StepUp™ Online Workbooks by following the instructions in "How to access the Lumos Online Workbooks" section of this chapter.
- Download the Lumos SchoolUp™ app using the instructions provided in the Lumos SchoolUp™ Mobile App FAQ section of this chapter to get useful school information.
- Review your child's performance in the "Lumos Online Workbooks" periodically. You can do this by simply asking your child to log into the system online and select the subject area you wish to review.
- Review your child's work in the practice PBA's and EOY's.

Teachers

- Please contact **support@lumoslearning.com** to request a **teacher account.** A teacher account will help you create custom assessments and lessons as well as review the online work of your students. Visit **http://www.lumoslearning.com/math-quill** to learn more.
- Download the Lumos SchoolUp™ app using the instructions provided in Lumos SchoolUp™ Mobile App FAQ to get convenient access to Common Core State Standards and additional school related resources.
- If your school has purchased the school edition of this book, please use this book as the Teacher Guide.
- You can use the Lumos online programs along with this book to complement and extend your classroom instruction.

PARCC Frequently Asked Questions

What Will PARCC Math Assessment Look Like?

For Math, PARCC differentiates three different types of questions:

Type I – Tasks assessing concepts, skills, procedures (Machine scorable only)
- Balance of conceptual understanding, fluency, and application
- Can involve any or all mathematical practice standards
- Machine scorable including innovative, computer-based formats
- Will appear on the End of Year and Performance Based Assessment components

Type II - Tasks assessing expressing mathematical reasoning
- Each task calls for written arguments/justifications, critique of reasoning or precision in mathematical statements (MP.3, 6).
- Can involve other mathematical practice standards
- May include a mix of machine-scored and hand-scored responses
- Included on the Performance Based Assessment component

Type III - Tasks assessing modeling/applications
- Each task calls for modeling/application in a real-world context or scenario (MP.4)
- Can involve other mathematical practice standards
- May include a mix of machine-scored and hand-scored responses
- Included on the Performance Based Assessment component

The PBA will be administered once 75% of the school year is complete. It will consist of Type I, Type II, and Type III questions. In the PBA, students will be given a set amount of time to complete their tasks.

The time for each PBA is described below:

Estimated Time on Task in Minutes (PBA)		
Grade	Session One	Session Two
3	50	50
4	50	50
5	50	50
6	50	50
7	50	50
8	50	50

The EOY will be administered once 90% of the school year is complete. It will consist of Type I questions only. In the EOY, students will also be given a set amount of time to complete their tasks.

The time for each EOY is described below:

Estimated Time on Task in Minutes (EOY)		
Grade	Session One	Session Two
3	55	55
4	55	55
5	55	55
6	55	55
7	55	55
8	55	55

What is a PARCC Aligned Test Practice Book?

Inside this book, you will find four full-length practice tests that are similar to the standardized tests students will take to assess their mastery of CCSS-aligned curriculum. Completing these tests will help students master the different areas that are included in newly aligned standardized tests and practice test taking skills. The results will help the students and educators get insights into students' strengths and weaknesses in specific content areas. These insights could be used to help students strengthen their skills in difficult topics and to improve speed and accuracy while taking the test.

How is this Lumos tedBook aligned to PARCC Guidelines?

Although the PARCC assessments will be conducted online, the practice tests here have been created to accurately reflect the depth and rigor of PARCC tasks in a pencil and paper format. Students will still be exposed to the Technology Enhanced Constructed-Response (TECR) style questions so they become familiar with the wording and how to think through these types of tasks.

This edition of the practice test book was created in the Summer 2014 and aligned to the most current PARCC standards released to date. Some changes will occur as PARCC continues to release new information in the fall of 2014 and beyond.

Where can I get more information about PARCC?

You can obtain up-to-date information on PARCC, including sample assessment items, schedules, & the answers to frequently asked questions from the PARCC website at **http://www.parcconline.org**

Where can I get additional information about the Common Core State Standards (CCSS)?

Please visit **http://www.corestandards.org/Math**

How to access the Lumos Online Workbooks

First Time Access:

Using a personal computer with internet access:	Using a smart phone or tablet:
Go to **http://www.lumoslearning.com/book**	Scan the QR Code below and follow the instructions.
Enter the following access code in the Access Code field and press the Submit button.	
Access Code: PG3M-524-63-P	

In the next screen, click on the "New User" button to register your user name and password.

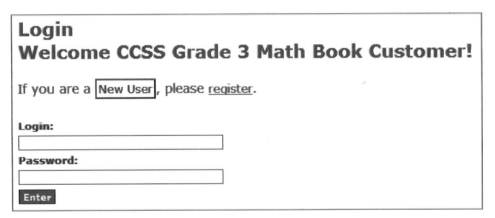

Login
Welcome CCSS Grade 3 Math Book Customer!

If you are a New User, please register.

Login:

Password:

Enter

Subsequent Access:

After you establish your user id and password for subsequent access, simply login with your account information.

What if I buy more than one Lumos Study Program?

Please note that you can use all Online Workbooks with one User ID and Password. If you buy more than one book, you will access them with the same account.

Go back to the **http://www.lumoslearning.com/book** link and enter the access code provided in the second book. In the next screen simply login using your previously created account.

Lumos StepUp™ Mobile App FAQ For Students

What is the Lumos StepUp™ App?

It is a FREE application you can download onto your Android smart phones, tablets, iPhones, and iPads.

What are the Benefits of the StepUp™ App?

This mobile application gives convenient access to Common Core State Standards, Practice Tests, Online Workbooks, and learning resources through your smart phone and tablet computers.

Do I Need the StepUp™ App to Access Online Workbooks?

No, you can access Lumos StepUp™ Online Workbooks through a personal computer. The StepUp™ app simply enhances your learning experience and allows you to conveniently access StepUp™ Online Workbooks and additional resources through your smart phone or tablet.

How can I Download the App?

Visit **lumoslearning.com/a/stepup-app** using your smart phone or tablet and follow the instructions to download the app.

QR Code
for Smart Phone
Or Tablet Users

Lumos SchoolUp™ Mobile App FAQ For Parents

What is the Lumos SchoolUp™ App?

It is a FREE App that helps parents and teachers get a wide range of useful information about their school. It can be downloaded onto smartphones and tablets from popular App Stores.

What are the Benefits of the Lumos SchoolUp™ App?

It provides convenient access to
- School performance reports.
- School "Stickies". A Sticky could be information about an upcoming test, homework, extra curricular activities and other school events. Parents and educators can easily create their own sticky and share with the school community.
- Common Core State Standards.
- Sample questions.
- Educational blogs.
- StepUp™ student activity reports.

How can I Download the App?

Visit **lumoslearning.com/a/schoolup-app** using your smartphone or tablet and follow the instructions provided to download the App. Alternatively, scan the QR Code provided below using your smartphone or tablet computer.

QR Code
for Smart Phone
Or Tablet Users

Is SchoolUp™ available for Apple Devices?

SchoolUp™ will be available for Apple devices in the future. The initial release is supported on the Android platform. However, users with iPhones or iPads can use the web version of SchoolUp™ by logging on to **lumoslearning.com/a/schoolup**

LumosLearning.com

Test Taking Tips

1) **The day before the test, make sure you get a good night's sleep.**

2) **On the day of the test, be sure to eat a good hearty breakfast! Also, be sure to arrive at school on time.**

3) **During the test:**

- **Read every question carefully.**

    - Do not spend too much time on any one question. Work steadily through all questions in the section.
    - Attempt all of the questions even if you are not sure of some answers.
    - If you run into a difficult question, eliminate as many choices as you can and then pick the best one from the remaining choices. Intelligent guessing will help you increase your score.
    - Also, mark the question so that if you have extra time, you can return to it after you reach the end of the section. Try to erase the marks after you complete the work.
    - Some questions may refer to a graph, chart, or other kind of picture. Carefully review the graphic before answering the question.
    - Be sure to include explanations for your written responses and show all work.

- **While Answering Multiple-Choice (EBSR) questions.**

    - Completely fill in the bubble corresponding to your answer choice.
    - Read all of the answer choices, even if think you have found the correct answer.

- **While Answering TECR questions.**

    - Read the directions of each question. Some might ask you to drag something, others to select, and still others to highlight. Follow all instructions of the question (or questions if it is in multiple parts)

Performance Based Assessment (PBA) - 1

Student Name: **Start Time:**
Test Date: **End Time:**

Here are some reminders for when you are taking the Grade 3 Mathematics Performance Based Assessment (PBA).

To answer the questions on the test, use the directions given in the question. If you do not know the answer to a question, skip it and go on to the next question. If time permits, you may return to questions in this session only. Do your best to answer every question.

---

1. **This beaker is holding 200 ml of water.**

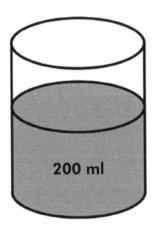

200 ml

PART A

How much water would there be if 8 beakers were each holding 200 ml of water? Write your answer in the box below.

           © Lumos Information Services 2014   LumosLearning.com   ▲

PART B

Suppose 100 ml were added to each of the beakers. Now how much water is present? Write your answer in the box below.

[ ]

PART C

Now, if 50 ml of water was poured out of one beaker, how much water would be left in the beakers, in the total? Write your answer in the box below.

[ ]

2. Write the correct number in the box to solve each equation.

$4 \times 6 =$ [ ]

$6 \times 3 =$ [ ]

$16 \div 4 =$ [ ]

$24 \div$ [ ] $= 8$

3. Which comparison symbol belongs in the blank?

$63 \div 9$ _____ $72 \div 8$

Ⓐ <
Ⓑ =
Ⓒ >

4. Audrey does 6 loads of laundry per week. How many loads of laundry are washed in 7 weeks?

   PART A

   First, write an equation letting L = total loads of laundry. Write your answer in the box below.

   ```



   ```

   PART B

   Now solve the equation: L = _____. Write your answer in the box below.

   ```



   ```

5. Grant scooped a pile of 24 bushels of wheat into the three bins of a grain drill for planting. He scooped the same amount into each bin How many bushels did he scoop into each bin? Write your answer in the box below.

   ```



   ```

6. If one piece of string pictured here is 8 inches long, how long would 9 strings be placed end to end?

   Write your answer in the box below.

   ```



   ```

LumosLearning.com

7. Pam shredded 3 blocks of cheese that were four pounds each for a dinner one evening.

   PART A

   How much cheese did she shred in all? Write your answer in the box below.

   [   ]

   PART B

   If 3 pounds were left out in the heat and spoiled, how much cheese was left? Write your answer in the box below.

   [   ]

8. Which letter (A, B or C) indicates the $\frac{2}{4}$ mark on the number line? Circle A, B or C.

   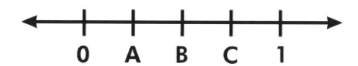

9. Kyle took a math test. Evaluate the following problem and answer to determine if he answered correctly.

   Kyle: $\frac{1}{2} + \frac{1}{2} = \frac{2}{4}$. Therefore $\frac{1}{2} + \frac{1}{2} + \frac{1}{2} + \frac{1}{2}$ which is equivalent to

   $\frac{2}{4} + \frac{2}{4} = 1$.

   PART A

   Where did Kyle figure incorrectly? Write your explanation in the box below.

   [   ]

PART B

How would you correct his mistake Write your explanation in the box below.

---

10. Terence decided to find out if it was less expensive to ride his bike to school or buy a skateboard to ride instead. Assume the bike would require 2 new tubes throughout the year as its only expense.

PART A

The price of 1 tube is $9.50. What is the price of 2 tubes? Write your answer in the box below.

PART B

The price of the skateboard is $22.00. Which would be a less costly means of transportation? Write your answer in the box below.

---

11. Beth was considering buying Paper Plate A for a party. The cost per bag of 200 was $4.00. She also considered Plate B which was $3.00 for a bag of 50.

Explain which type would be less costly and why. Write your explanation in the box below.

12. On the number line below, divide the space between 1 and 2 into eighths.

13. The clock below displays a time that is 15 minutes before Kim's favorite television show.

PART A

What time does Kim's show start? Write your answer in the box below.

PART B

What time will it be when Kim is through watching her 30 minute show? Write your answer in the box below.

```
+---------------------------------------------+
|                                             |
+---------------------------------------------+
```

14. Betty arranges cupcakes on the shelf to cool. She has 72 of them. If she has enough space to put 8 in a row, how would you determine how many rows she will need? Write your explanation in the box below.

```
+---------------------------------------------------+
|                                                   |
|                                                   |
|                                                   |
|                                                   |
|                                                   |
|                                                   |
+---------------------------------------------------+
```

15. Farmer Jake owned 91 goats and 139 pigs. How could you use estimation to estimate about how many animals are on his farm? Write your explanation in the box below.

```
+---------------------------------------------------+
|                                                   |
|                                                   |
|                                                   |
|                                                   |
|                                                   |
+---------------------------------------------------+
```

LumosLearning.com   ▲

16. **Which three of the following fractions make this expression true? Fill in the bubble corresponding to your answer choice.**

$$\frac{1}{2} = \underline{\hspace{1cm}}$$

Ⓐ 1

Ⓑ $\frac{3}{6}$

Ⓒ $\frac{5}{2}$

Ⓓ $\frac{2}{4}$

Ⓔ $\frac{4}{8}$

17.

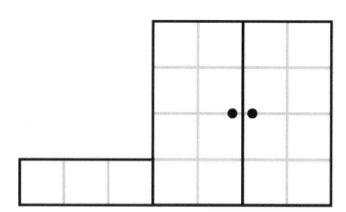

= 1 sq. ft.

PART A

Count the squares to determine the area of this closet. Write your answer in the box below.

PART B

If the closet was twice as large, how many square feet would it have? Write your answer in the box below.

```
┌────────────────────────────────────────────┐
│                                            │
│                                            │
└────────────────────────────────────────────┘
```

End of Performance Based Assessment (PBA) - 1

LumosLearning.com   ▲

Performance Based Assessment (PBA) - 1

Answer Key

Question No.	Answer	Related Lumos Online Workbook	CCSS
1 PART A	1,600 ml	Applying Multiplication & Division	3.OA.3
1 PART B	2,400 ml	Applying Multiplication & Division	3.OA.3
1 PART C	2,350 ml	Applying Multiplication & Division	3.OA.3
2 PART A	24	Multiplication & Division Facts	3.OA.7
2 PART B	18	Multiplication & Division Facts	3.OA.7
2 PART C	4	Multiplication & Division Facts	3.OA.7
2 PART D	3	Multiplication & Division Facts	3.OA.7
3	A	Multiplication & Division Facts	3.OA.7
4 PART A	6 loads x 7 weeks = L or 6 x 7 = L	Understanding Multiplication	3.OA.1
4 PART B	L = 6 x 7 = 42	Understanding Multiplication	3.OA.1
5	8	Applying Multiplication & Division; Finding Unknown Values	3.OA.3-4
6	72 inches	Applying Multiplication & Division; Finding Unknown Values	3.OA.3-2
7 PART A	12 pounds	Applying Multiplication & Division; Finding Unknown Values	3.OA.3-1
7 PART B	9 pounds	Applying Multiplication & Division; Finding Unknown Values	3.OA.3-1
8	B	Fractions on the Number Line	3.NF.2
9 PART A	*	Equivalent Fractions	3.NF.3
9 PART B	*	Equivalent Fractions	3.NF.3
10 PART A	$19.00	Two-Step Problems	3.D.1
10 PART B	Bicycle	Two-Step Problems	3.OA.8
11	A plates	Two-Step Problems	3.OA.8
12	*	Fractions on the Number Line	3.NF.2
13 PART A	3:00	Telling Time	3.MD.1
13 PART B	3:30	Telling Time	3.MD.1
14	*	Understanding Division	3.OA.2
15	*	Rounding Numbers	3.NBT.1

Question No.	Answer	Related Lumos Online Workbook	CCSS
16	B, D, and E	Comparing Fractions; Equivalent Fractions	3.NF.3b-1
17 PART A	19 sq. ft.	Area	3.MD.6
17 PART B	38 sq. ft.	Area	3.MD.6

* **See detailed explanation**

Performance Based Assessment (PBA) - 1

Detailed Explanations

Question No.	Answer	Detailed Explanation
1 PART A	1,600 ml	Multiply the first number and place the correct number of zeroes after your answer.
1 PART B	2,400 ml	8 x 100= 800 ml. Next add 800 to 1,600 to arrive at 2,400.
1 PART C	2,350 ml	2,400-50=2,350
2 PART A	24	Approach each of these as a multiplication problem. Think "What number times the number given will arrive at the product?"
2 PART B	18	Approach each of these as a multiplication problem. Think "What number times the number given will arrive at the product?"
2 PART C	4	Approach each of these as a multiplication problem. Think "What number times the number given will arrive at the product?"
2 PART D	3	Approach each of these as a multiplication problem. Think "What number times the number given will arrive at the product?"
3	A	The left side is less than the right side. The "less than" sign is needed. 7< 9
4 PART A	6 loads x 7 weeks = L or 6 x 7 = L	
4 PART B	L = 6 x 7 = 42	This is a multiplication fact to be memorized.
5	8	24 ÷ **8** =3 He scooped 8 bushels into each bin. 3 x 8 = 24. Approach division as a multiplication problem.
6	72 inches	8 x 9 = **72** inches. This a standard fact to be memorized.
7 PART A	12 pounds	3 x 4 = **12** pounds.
7 PART B	9 pounds	12-3 = **9** pounds.

Question No.	Answer	Detailed Explanation
8	B	It is half way between 0 and 1. $$\frac{2}{4} = \frac{1}{2}$$
9 PART A		By common sense one should see that two halves make a whole, not another half. When adding fractions, keep the denominator constant.
9 PART B		When adding fractions, keep the denominator constant.
10 PART A	$19.00	Approach this as a multiplication problem. 2 x 9.50 = $19.00
10 PART B	Bicycle	Compare the two prices. $19.00 < $22.00
11	A plates	The cost of $4.00 divided by 200 is $.02 per plate. $3.00 divided by 50 is $.06 per plate. Therefore the A plates are less costly.
12		All the marks should be between 1 and 2.
13 PART A	3:00	2:45 is the time shown on the clock. Add to that 15 minutes and you have 3:00
13 PART B	3:30	If her show starts at 3:00, add 30 minutes to that. Her show ends at 3:30.
14		Approach this as a multiplication or a division problem. 8 x ___ = 72 or 72 ÷ 8 = ___. The missing number is 9. There should be 9 rows.
15		91 is rounded down to estimate 90. 139 is rounded up to estimate 140. Add 90 and 140 to arrive at 230. This will be close to the correct answer, as we just rounded.

LumosLearning.com

Question No.	Answer	Detailed Explanation
16	B, D, and E	The numerator, when multiplied by 2, should equal the denominator.
17 PART A	19 sq. ft.	
17 PART B	38 sq. ft.	If the closet was twice as large, how many square feet would it have? 19 x 2 = 38 sq. feet

Notes

LumosLearning.com

Performance Based Assessment (PBA) - 2

Student Name: **Start Time:**
Test Date: **End Time:**

Here are some reminders for when you are taking the Grade 3 Mathematics Performance Based Assessment (PBA).

To answer the questions on the test, use the directions given in the question. If you do not know the answer to a question, skip it and go on to the next question. If time permits, you may return to questions in this session only. Do your best to answer every question.

---

1. Robert shoveled dirt into five different piles. Each pile consisted of nine scoops. What is the total number of scoops of dirt?

   PART A

   First write an equation letting s = the number of scoops. Write your answer in the box below.

   ```



   ```

   PART B

   Now solve the equation: s = _____ . Write your answer in the box below.

   ```



   ```

2. Clarissa was giving away clothing items that were too small for her. She had three cousins with whom she was sharing the clothing. If Clarissa had 27 pieces of clothing and shared equally with all cousins, how many items did each cousin receive? Write your answer in the box below.

   ```



   ```

3. Julie needed 9 ounces of potato salad to feed each of her 9 guests at a picnic. How many ounces did she need in all? Write your answer in the box below.

4. Mark and his brothers worked together to pick tomatoes. Each of the 4 boys picked 8 pounds.

    PART A

    How many pounds did they pick in all?

    4 x 8 = P, P= pounds of tomatoes. P=_____. Write your answer in the box below.

    PART B

    If 7 pounds were used for the family dinner that night, how many pounds of tomatoes remained? Write your answer in the box below.

5. Which letter (A or B) indicates the $\frac{1}{3}$ mark on the number line? Circle A or B on the number line.

6. Carter added fractions. He determined that $\frac{3}{3} + \frac{4}{4} = 7$. His reasoning was that $\frac{3}{3} = 3$ and $\frac{4}{4} = 4$. $3 + 4 = 7$.

PART A

Can you find what he did incorrectly? Write your explanation in the box below.

PART B

What answer would you have for $\frac{3}{3} + \frac{4}{4} =$ _____? Write your answer in the box below.

7. Christine noticed that students who used Scribbles brand of crayons were having more trouble with them breaking than those who used Brighter brand of crayons. In fact the students with Scribbles brand used an average of 3 boxes per year, where the others used only 1 box.

PART A

The price of 1 box of Scribbles was $2.00. What is the price of 3 boxes? Write your answer in the box below.

The price of 1 box of Brighter brand was $4.00. Which type of crayons cost more money for the student's family for one year? Write your answer in the box below.

8. Lawnmower A requires $10 of maintenance a year but uses half the gas of Lawnmower B. Which mower is a less expensive piece of equipment to run if Lawnmower B requires only a $5 maintenance? Assume that about $200 worth of gas would be needed for Lawnmower B. Write your answer in the box below.

9. On the number line below, divide the space between 0 and 1 into sixths.

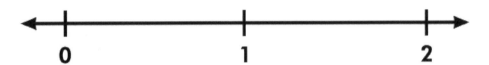

10. The clock below displays a time that is 20 minutes past Todd's bedtime.

PART A

What time does Todd go to bed? Write your answer in the box below.

PART B

What time would it be if Todd is 30 minutes late getting to bed? Write your answer in the box below.

```



```

11. Aaron cleaned his room and arranged books on a shelf. In all, he had 63 books. He had 7 shelves on which to place them. How would you determine how many books will be on each shelf? Write your explanation in the box below.

```




```

12. 38 boys and 241 girls attended a picnic. How could you use estimation to arrive at an answer that is very close to the exact number in attendance? Write your explanation in the box below.

```




```

13. **Which three of the following fractions make this comparison true? Fill in the bubble corresponding to your answer choice.**

$$\frac{1}{4} = \underline{\hspace{1.5cm}}$$

Ⓐ 1

Ⓑ $\frac{2}{8}$

Ⓒ $\frac{3}{12}$

Ⓓ $\frac{2}{4}$

Ⓔ $\frac{4}{16}$

14.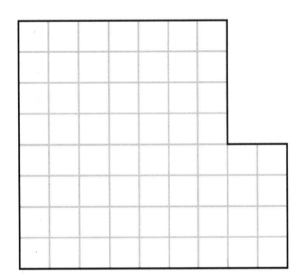

□ = 1 sq. ft.

PART A

Count the squares to determine the area of this room.
Write your answer in the box below.

PART B

If the room was only half as large, how many square feet would it cover? Write your answer in the box below.

```
[                                        ]
```

15. This bottle is holding 300 ml of milk.

PART A

How much milk would there be if 8 bottles were each holding 300 ml of milk? Write your answer in the box below.

```
[                                        ]
```

PART B

Suppose 200 ml were added to each of the bottles. Now how much milk is present? Write your answer in the box below.

```
[                                        ]
```

PART C

Now, if we add an additional 100 ml of milk to one bottle, how much milk is present? Write your answer in the box below.

```
[                                        ]
```

16. **Supply the missing number to make each equation correct.**

    5 x 6 = ⬚

    9 x 3 = ⬚

    16 ÷ 8 = ⬚

    36 ÷ ⬚ = 6

17. **Which symbol belongs in the blank?**

    35 ÷ 5 _____ 56 ÷ 8

    Ⓐ <
    Ⓑ =
    Ⓒ >

End of Performance Based Assessment (PBA) - 2

     LumosLearning.com   ▼

Performance Based Assessment (PBA) - 2

Answer Key

Question No.	Answer	Related Lumos Online Workbook	CCSS
1 PART A	*	Understanding Multiplication	3.OA.1
1 PART B	45 scoops	Understanding Multiplication	3.OA.1
2	9 items	Applying Multiplication & Division; Finding Unknown Values	3.OA.3-4
3	81 ounces	Applying Multiplication & Division; Understanding Division	3.OA.3-2
4 PART A	32 pounds	Two-Step Problems; Multiplication & Division Facts; Relating Multiplication & Division; Multiplication & Division Properties; Finding Unknown Values; Applying Multiplication & Division; Understanding Division; Understanding Multiplication	3.OA.8-1
4 PART B	25 pounds	Two-Step Problems; Multiplication & Division Facts; Relating Multiplication & Division; Multiplication & Division Properties; Finding Unknown Values; Applying Multiplication & Division; Understanding Division; Understanding Multiplication	3.OA.8-1
5	A	Fractions on the Number Line	3.NF.2
6 PART A	*	Equivalent Fractions	3.NF.3
6 PART B	2	Equivalent Fractions	3.NF.3
7 PART A	$6.00	Applying Multiplication & Division	3.OA.3
7 PART B	Scribbles	Applying Multiplication & Division	3.OA.3
8	Lawnmower A	Two-Step Problems	3.OA.8
9	*	Fractions on the Number Line	3.NF.2
10 PART A	8:00 PM	Telling Time	3.MD.1
10 PART B	8:30 PM	Telling Time	3.MD.1
11	*	Understanding Division	3.OA.2
12	*	Rounding Numbers	3.NBT.1

Question No.	Answer	Related Lumos Online Workbook	CCSS
13 PART A	B, C, and E	Comparing Fractions	3.NF.3b-1
14 PART A	64 sq. ft.	Area	3.MD.5-7
14 PART B	32 sq. ft.	Area	3.MD.5-7
15 PART A	2,400ml	Applying Multiplication & Division	3.OA.3
15 PART B	4,000 ml	Applying Multiplication & Division	3.OA.3
15 PART C	4,100 ml	Applying Multiplication & Division	3.OA.3
16 PART A	30	Multiplication & Division Facts	3.OA.7
16 PART B	27	Multiplication & Division Facts	3.OA.7
16 PART C	2	Multiplication & Division Facts	3.OA.7
16 PART D	6	Multiplication & Division Facts	3.OA.7
17	B	Multiplication & Division Facts	3.OA.7

* See detailed explanation

Performance Based Assessment (PBA) - 2

Detailed Explanations

Question No.	Answer	Detailed Explanation
1 PART A		5 piles x 9 scoops = s or 5 x 9 = s
1 PART B	45 scoops	s= 45 scoops 5 x 9 is a multiplication fact to memorize.
2	9 items	27÷3=9 Think, "What number when multiplied by 3 equals 27?"
3	81 ounces	9 x 9 =81 ounces. 9 x 9 is a multiplication fact to be memorized.
4 PART A	32 pounds	4 x 8 = P, P= pounds of tomatoes. P= 32 pounds
4 PART B	25 pounds	32- 7 = 25 pounds
5	A	
6 PART A		Carter should have realized that when the numerator and denominator are the same, the fraction is equivalent to 1, not the number listed for the numerator and denominator. Therefore, the answer is 2.
6 PART B	2	
7 PART A	$6.00	$2.00 x 3 boxes = $6.00 This is a standard multiplication fact.
7 PART B	Scribbles	Even though 1 box of scribbles was less expensive, the necessity of purchasing more boxes was more costly. $6.00 > $4.00
8	Lawnmower A	Lawnmower A would be less expensive, taking gas into consideration. It would not take long to use the $5 difference in maintenance for the mower using more gas.

Question No.	Answer	Detailed Explanation
9		All marks should all be between 0 and 1.
10 PART A	8:00 PM	The time on the clock is 8:00 PM.
10 PART B	8:30 PM	Add 30 minutes to Todd's typical bedtime of 8:00 and the total is 8:30. Think of it as an addition problem. 8:00 + 0:30 = 8:30
11		This is a division problem. However, it can be approached as multiplication. Just figure what number needs to be multiplied by 7 to arrive at 63. The missing number is 9.
12		This is a multi-step problem. First, round 38 to 40 and 241 to 240. Then 40 + 240 = 280. 280 should be a close estimate.
13 PART A	B, C, and E	The numerator multiplied by 4 must equal the denominator.
14 PART A	64 sq. ft.	
14 PART B	32 sq. ft.	Divide 64 in half. Think of it as 64 ÷ 2 = 32

LumosLearning.com   ▼

Question No.	Answer	Detailed Explanation
15 PART A	2,400ml	Multiply the first numbers, 8 x 3= 24, then place the given number of zeroes after the answer.
15 PART B	4,000 ml	First, find the total amount of milk added to the bottles. 8 x 200 = 1,600. Then, add that total to the amount of milk already present. 2400 + 1600= 4,000
15 PART C	4,100 ml	4,000 + 100 = 4,100. We are just adding milk to one of the bottles. Not all of the bottles.
16 PART A	30	Approach each of these as a multiplication problem. Think "What number times the number given will arrive at the product?"
16 PART B	27	Approach each of these as a multiplication problem. Think "What number times the number given will arrive at the product?"
16 PART C	2	Approach each of these as a multiplication problem. Think "What number times the number given will arrive at the product?"
16 PART D	6	Approach each of these as a multiplication problem. Think "What number times the number given will arrive at the product?"
17	B	Look at the problem and decide if the left or right side greater, or are they equal?

Notes

© Lumos Information Services 2014   LumosLearning.com

End-Of-Year Assessment (EOY) - 1

Student Name: Start Time:
Test Date: End Time:

Here are some reminders for when you are taking the Grade 3 Mathematics End-Of-Year Assessment (EOY).

To answer the questions on the test, use the directions given in the question. If you do not know the answer to a question, skip it and go on to the next question. If time permits, you may return to questions in this session only. Do your best to answer every question.

1. **Supply the missing factor, product or quotient for each equation.**

   5 x 7 = ☐

   49 ÷ 7 = ☐

   ☐ x 6 = 24

   72 ÷ 9 = ☐

2. **PART A**

   Caden jogs 8 miles per day. How many miles will he travel in 30 days? Write your answer in the box below.

PART B

Caden usually jogs 720 miles in 90 days. However, there were three rainy days when he did not run. How many miles did he run in the 90 days. Write your answer in the box below.

3. Record the measurement of this piece of string to the nearest $\frac{1}{4}$ inch.

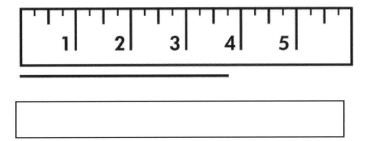

4. Jerry collected 997 rocks over 5 years. After he gave some to his brother, he only had 818 left. How many did he give to his brother? Write your answer in the box below.

5. Which boxes are $\frac{3}{4}$ full? Fill in the bubble corresponding to your answer choice.

Ⓐ

Ⓑ

Ⓒ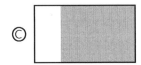

Ⓓ

    LumosLearning.com

6. **What is the area of each figure shown?**

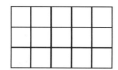 _____ sq. units

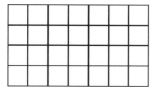 _____ sq. units

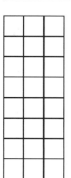 _____ sq. units

7. **40 horses were divided equally among 4 barns. How many horses stayed in each barn? Write your answer in the box below.**

8. **Which of the following shows the sum of 354 + 412 in expanded form?**

    Ⓐ **700+70+6**
    Ⓑ **700+60+6**
    Ⓒ **700+700+60**
    Ⓓ **7000+600+60**

9. **Supply the missing factor, product or quotient for each equation.**

    6 x 3 = ☐

    5 x ☐ = 45

    36 ÷ 6 = ☐

    7 x ☐ = 63

10. **Which three are examples of quadrilaterals? Fill in the bubble corresponding to your answer choice.**

Ⓐ

Ⓑ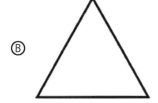

Ⓒ

Ⓓ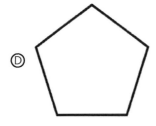

Ⓔ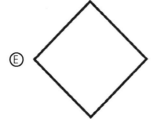

          LumosLearning.com   ◀

11. The clock shows the time that Katie starts her afternoon piano lesson.

PART A

If she finishes 45 minutes later, what time will it be then?

Ⓐ 3:15 P.M.
Ⓑ 4:30 P.M.
Ⓒ 4:45 P.M.
Ⓓ 3:45 P.M.

PART B

Katie's teacher uses the last ten minutes to practice music theory on the computer. What time did Katie start working on the computer? Write your answer in the box below.

```
┌─────────────────────────────────────────────┐
│                                             │
│                                             │
└─────────────────────────────────────────────┘
```

12. Which three of the following represent the expression 6 x 7? Fill in the bubble corresponding to your answer choice.

Ⓐ six groups of seven trees
Ⓑ six apples and seven oranges
Ⓒ seven peaches, six get eaten
Ⓓ six children in a group, seven groups
Ⓔ seven groups of six toys

13. Which three of the following numbers make this equation true?

$$\frac{5}{5} = \underline{\hspace{2cm}}$$

Ⓐ 1

Ⓑ $\frac{6}{6}$

Ⓒ $\frac{5}{2}$

Ⓓ $\frac{4}{4}$

Ⓔ 5

14. Which comparison symbol belongs in the blank?

$$20 \div 5 \underline{\hspace{2cm}} 24 \div 6$$

Ⓐ <
Ⓑ =
Ⓒ >

15. Place the missing number in the blank.

$60 \times 10 = \boxed{}$

$50 \times \boxed{} = 450$

$\boxed{} \times 8 = 240$

LumosLearning.com

16. The graph below shows the number of each type of tree growing in a city park. Complete the following exercises based on this information.

Trees

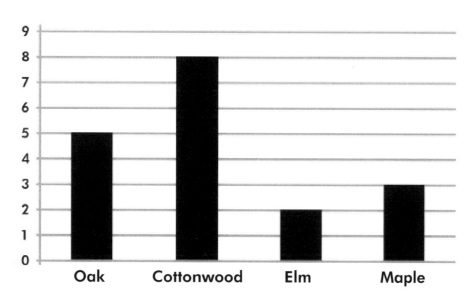

■ Variety

PART A

There are _____ times the number of cottonwood trees as there are elm trees. Write your answer in the box below.

PART B

How many more maple trees are there than elm trees? Write your answer in the box below.

PART C

The number of cottonwood trees equals the number of _____ and _____ trees together. Write your answers in the box below.

17. **Mark the two of the following shapes that have at least one pair of parallel sides.**

　Ⓐ

　Ⓑ

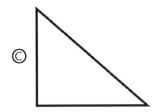　Ⓒ

　Ⓓ

18. **Which of the following diagrams represents the fraction $\frac{2}{4}$? _____**

Ⓐ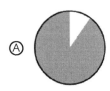

Ⓑ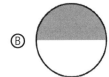

Ⓒ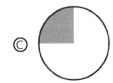

Ⓓ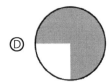

　© Lumos Information Services 2014　　LumosLearning.com

19. On the graph below, shade in the squares to indicate 30 hours of reading time. Each section equals 5 hours.

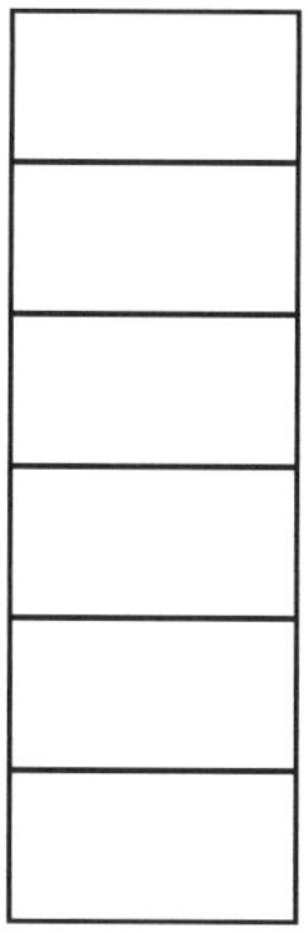

Time spent reading

5 hours

20. Supply the missing number in each equation.

6 x [ ] = 54

9 x 9 = [ ]

[ ] x 8 = 24

21. Larry grows tomatoes to sell. From the first three days he picked tomatoes he gathered this many pounds: 58 pounds, 69 pounds, and 145 pounds. 19 pounds rotted before he could sell them.

PART A

Assuming Larry sold all of the rest of the tomatoes, what was the total amount of tomatoes he sold the first three days? Write your answer in the box below.

[ ]

PART B

The second week Larry picked only 6 pounds each day for 4 days. For the next 3 days an equal number of tomatoes was sold until all of those tomatoes were gone. How many pounds of tomatoes were sold per day? Write your answer in the box below.

22. Supply the correct answer in the space.

$48 \div 6 = \boxed{}$

$5 \times 6 = \boxed{}$

$4 \times \boxed{} = 32$

$\boxed{} \times 7 = 42$

$45 \div \boxed{} = 9$

23. Based on the picture below, which of the following statements are true?

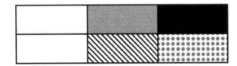

Ⓐ $\dfrac{2}{6}$ of the figure is not colored

Ⓑ $\dfrac{3}{6}$ of the figure is colored

Ⓒ $\dfrac{2}{6}$ of the figure is black or dotted

Ⓓ $\dfrac{2}{3}$ of the figure is colored

Ⓔ $\dfrac{1}{3}$ of the figure is striped

 LumosLearning.com

24. Find the difference. Place the answer in the box.

839 - 67 = ☐

25. Estimate each difference by rounding each number to the nearest 10.

PART A

38 - 12 = ☐

PART B

139 - 21 = ☐

26. Ross gathered eggs each morning. He gathered 3 eggs everyday for 8 days.

PART A

How many eggs did he gather in all? Write your answer in the box below.

☐

PART B

Ross divided all the eggs gathered into egg cartons that hold 6 eggs each. How many cartons did he use? Write your answer in the box below.

☐

27. Divide the square into six equal sections and shade $\frac{1}{6}$.

28. All sides are marked except one.

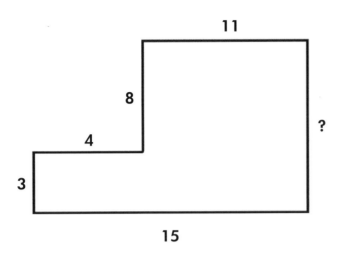

What is the missing length if the perimeter is 52cm? Write your answer in the box below.

29. Below you will find an image of a rectangle with length 8 inches and width 4 inches.

What is the total area of this rectangle? Write your answer in the box below.

30. **Supply the missing factor, product or quotient for each equation.**

4 x 7 = ☐

6 x ☐ = 36

56 ÷ 8 = ☐

8 x 8 = ☐

31. **What is the perimeter of a square building that is 8 feet on a side? Write your answer in the box below.**

☐

32. **Which of the following pictures represent 6 x 7? Fill in the bubble corresponding to your answer choice.**

Ⓐ

Ⓓ

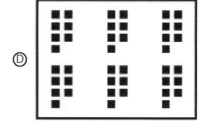

Ⓑ

Ⓔ

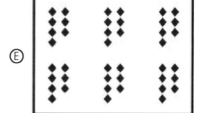

Ⓒ

33. Find $\dfrac{8}{8}$ on the number line.

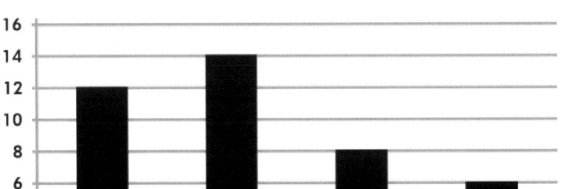

34. The chart below shows the number of each type of cats in a city park. Complete the following exercises based on this information.

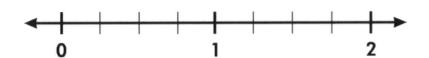

Cats

■ Cats

PART A

How many times the number of white cats are the yellow cats? Write your answer in the box below.

© Lumos Information Services 2014   LumosLearning.com

PART B

How many less calico cats are there than grey cats? Write your answer in the box below.

[   ]

PART C

What is the total number of cats represented? Write your answer in the box below.

[   ]

35. There are 6 rows of 9 apple trees in the orchard. How many trees are there in the orchard in all? Write your answer in the box below.

[   ]

36. There are 36 grams of cereal in an unopened box. Jeremy eats one bowl of 7 grams of cereal. How many grams are left in the box? Write your answer in the box below.

[   ]

37. A small auditorium has 9 rows of 8 seats per row. How many people can be seated in the auditorium if all seats are filled? Write your answer in the box below.

[   ]

38. Plot an equivalent fraction on the second number line.

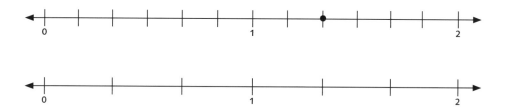

39. Select the term that makes each sentence correct.

PART A

A rhombus is a parallelogram.

Ⓐ TRUE
Ⓑ FALSE

PART B

A square is a rhombus.

Ⓐ TRUE
Ⓑ FALSE

End of End-Of-Year Assessment (EOY) - 1

LumosLearning.com

End-Of-Year Assessment (EOY) -1

Answer Key

Question No.	Answer	Related Lumos Online Workbook	CCSS
1 PART A	35	Multiplication & Division Facts; Relating Multiplication & Division; Multiplication & Division Properties; Finding Unknown Values; Applying Multiplication & Division; Understanding Division	3.OA.7-2
1 PART B	7	Multiplication & Division Facts; Relating Multiplication & Division; Multiplication & Division Properties; Finding Unknown Values; Applying Multiplication & Division; Understanding Division	3.OA.7-2
1 PART C	4	Multiplication & Division Facts; Relating Multiplication & Division; Multiplication & Division Properties; Finding Unknown Values; Applying Multiplication & Division; Understanding Division	3.OA.7-2
1 PART D	8	Multiplication & Division Facts; Relating Multiplication & Division; Multiplication & Division Properties; Finding Unknown Values; Applying Multiplication & Division; Understanding Division	3.OA.7-2
2 PART A	240 miles	Multiplying Multiples of 10	3.NBT.3
2 PART B	696 miles	Addition & Subtraction	3.Int.5
3	*	Measuring Length	3.MD.4
4	179 rocks	Addition & Subtraction	3.NBT.2
5	A and C	Fractions of a Whole	3.NF.1
6	15, 28 and 24 sq. units	Area	3.MD.5-7
7	10 horses	Multiplying Multiples of 10	3.NBT.3
8	B	Addition & Subtraction	3.NBT.2
9 PART A	18	Multiplication & Division Facts	3.OA.7
9 PART B	9	Multiplication & Division Facts	3.OA.7
9 PART C	6	Multiplication & Division Facts	3.OA.7

Question No.	Answer	Related Lumos Online Workbook	CCSS
9 PART D	9	Multiplication & Division Facts	3.OA.7
10	A, C, E	2-Dimensional Shapes	3.G.1
11 PART A	C	Elapsed Time	3.MD.1
11 PART B	4:35 P.M.	Elapsed Time	3.MD.1
12	A, D, E	Understanding Multiplication	3.OA.1
13	A, B, D	Equivalent Fractions	3.NF.3
14	B	Multiplication & Division Facts	3.OA.7
15 PART A	600	Multiplying Multiples of 10	3.NBT.3
15 PART B	9	Multiplying Multiples of 10	3.NBT.3
15 PART C	30	Multiplying Multiples of 10	3.NBT.3
16 PART A	4	Graphs	3.MD.3
16 PART B	1	Graphs	3.MD.3
16 PART C	The number of cottonwood trees equals the number of oak and maple trees together.	Graphs	3.MD.3
17	A, B	2-Dimensional Shapes	3.G.1
18	B	Fractions of a Whole	3.NF.1
19	*	Graphs	3.MD.3
20 PART A	9	Multiplication & Division Facts; Relating Multiplication & Division; Multiplication & Division Properties; Finding Unknown Values; Applying Multiplication & Division; Understanding Division	3.OA.7-2
20 PART B	81	Multiplication & Division Facts; Relating Multiplication & Division; Multiplication & Division Properties; Finding Unknown Values; Applying Multiplication & Division; Understanding Division	3.OA.7-2
20 PART C	3	Multiplication & Division Facts; Relating Multiplication & Division; Multiplication & Division Properties; Finding Unknown Values; Applying Multiplication & Division; Understanding Division	3.OA.7-2
21 PART A	253 pounds	Addition & Subtraction	3.NBT.2

 LumosLearning.com ◀

Question No.	Answer	Related Lumos Online Workbook	CCSS
21 PART B	8 pounds	Applying Multiplication & Division	3.OA.3
22 PART A	8	Multiplication & Division Facts; Relating Multiplication & Division; Multiplication & Division Properties; Finding Unknown Values; Applying Multiplication & Division; Understanding Division	3.OA.7-2
22 PART B	30	Multiplication & Division Facts; Relating Multiplication & Division; Multiplication & Division Properties; Finding Unknown Values; Applying Multiplication & Division; Understanding Division	3.OA.7-2
22 PART C	8	Multiplication & Division Facts; Relating Multiplication & Division; Multiplication & Division Properties; Finding Unknown Values; Applying Multiplication & Division; Understanding Division	3.OA.7-2
22 PART D	6	Multiplication & Division Facts; Relating Multiplication & Division; Multiplication & Division Properties; Finding Unknown Values; Applying Multiplication & Division; Understanding Division	3.OA.7-2
22 PART E	5	Multiplication & Division Facts; Relating Multiplication & Division; Multiplication & Division Properties; Finding Unknown Values; Applying Multiplication & Division; Understanding Division	3.OA.7-2
23	A, C, D	Fractions of a Whole	3.NF.1
24	772	Addition & Subtraction	3.NBT.2
25 PART A	30	Rounding Numbers	3.NBT.1
25 PART B	120	Rounding Numbers	3.NBT.1
26 PART A	24	Two-Step Problems; Multiplication & Division Facts; Relating Multiplication & Division; Multiplication & Division Properties; Finding Unknown Values; Applying Multiplication & Division; Understanding Division; Understanding Multiplication	3.OA.8.1

Question No.	Answer	Related Lumos Online Workbook	CCSS
26 PART B	4 cartons	Two-Step Problems; Multiplication & Division Facts; Relating Multiplication & Division; Multiplication & Division Properties; Finding Unknown Values; Applying Multiplication & Division; Understanding Division; Understanding Multiplication	3.OA.8.1
27	*	Shape Partitions	3.G.2
28	11 cm	Perimeter	3.MD.8
29	32 square inches	Area; Measuring Length; Graphs; Liquid Volume & Mass; Elapsed Time	3.MD.7-1
30 PART A	28	Finding Unknown Values	3.OA.4
30 PART B	6	Finding Unknown Values	3.OA.4
30 PART C	7	Finding Unknown Values	3.OA.4
30 PART D	64	Finding Unknown Values	3.OA.4
31	32 feet	Perimeter	3.MD.8
32	B, D, E	Understanding Multiplication	3.OA.1
33	*	Fractions on the Number Line	3.NF.2
34 PART A	$2\frac{1}{3}$ times	Graphs	3.MD.3
34 PART B	4	Graphs	3.MD.3
34 PART C	40 cats	Graphs	3.MD.3
35	54 trees	Applying Multiplication & Division; Understanding Division; Understanding Multiplication	3.OA.3-1
36	29 grams	Liquid Volume & Mass	3.MD.2-2
37	72 people	Applying Multiplication & Division	3.OA.3-3
38	*	Comparing Fractions; Fractions on the Number Line	3.NF.3A-2
39 PART A	true	2-Dimensional Shapes	3.G.1
39 PART B	true	2-Dimensional Shapes	3.G.1

* See detailed explanation

End-Of-Year Assessment (EOY) - 1

Detailed Explanations

Question No.	Answer	Detailed Explanation
1 PART A	35	When completing division problems, think of the unknown factor to approach it like a multiplication problem. Think, "What number, when multiplied by the given factor, equals the product?" All multiplication tables from 1-10 need to be memorized until they are automatic.
1 PART B	7	When completing division problems, think of the unknown factor to approach it like a multiplication problem. Think, "What number, when multiplied by the given factor, equals the product?" All multiplication tables from 1-10 need to be memorized until they are automatic.
1 PART C	4	When completing division problems, think of the unknown factor to approach it like a multiplication problem. Think, "What number, when multiplied by the given factor, equals the product?" All multiplication tables from 1-10 need to be memorized until they are automatic.
1 PART D	8	When completing division problems, think of the unknown factor to approach it like a multiplication problem. Think, "What number, when multiplied by the given factor, equals the product?" All multiplication tables from 1-10 need to be memorized until they are automatic.
2 PART A	240 miles	This problem can be solved by multiplying the first two digits and then adding a 0. So, 8x3=24 and add a 0 to be 240.
2 PART B	696 miles	We should quickly see that 90 x 8= 720. 8 x 3 are the number of miles he did not run due to rainy days. 720-24= 696.
3		 $3 \frac{3}{4}$ inches is the result. Each mark represents $\frac{1}{4}$ inch.

Question No.	Answer	Detailed Explanation
4	179 rocks	Starting with 997, subtract 818. The difference is 179. When subtracting, be sure to line up the place values vertically (ones, tens, hundreds).
5	A and C	A and C are $\frac{3}{4}$ full as each mark indicates $\frac{1}{4}$.
6	15, 28 and 24 sq. units	3 x 5 = 15 sq units 4 x 7 = 28 sq units 8 x 3 = 24 sq units
7	10 horses	40 ÷ 4 = 10. When completing division problems, think of the unknown factor to approach it like a multiplication problem. What number, when multiplied by the given factor, equals the product? All multiplication tables from 1-10 need to be memorized until they are automatic.
8	B	We arrive at 766 when the numbers are added. In expanded form, the value of 100's, 10's, and 1's are all listed separately with an addition sign between them.
9 PART A	18	When completing division problems, think of the unknown factor and approach it like a multiplication problem. What number, when multiplied by the given factor, equals the product? All multiplication tables from 1-10 need to be memorized until they are automatic.
9 PART B	9	When completing division problems, think of the unknown factor and approach it like a multiplication problem. What number, when multiplied by the given factor, equals the product? All multiplication tables from 1-10 need to be memorized until they are automatic.

Question No.	Answer	Detailed Explanation
9 PART C	6	When completing division problems, think of the unknown factor and approach it like a multiplication problem. What number, when multiplied by the given factor, equals the product? All multiplication tables from 1-10 need to be memorized until they are automatic.
9 PART D	9	When completing division problems, think of the unknown factor and approach it like a multiplication problem. What number, when multiplied by the given factor, equals the product? All multiplication tables from 1-10 need to be memorized until they are automatic.
10	A, C, E	A, C, E each have four sides. The definition of quadrilateral requires four sides exactly.
11 PART A	C	The time on the clock is 4:00. If you add 45 minutes to that time, to account for the lesson, you will see she finishes at 4:45.
11 PART B	4:35 P.M.	4:45-10=4:35 Subtract the 10 from the minutes portion of the time. 45-10=35.
12	A, D, E	
13	A, B, D	As long as the numerator and denominator are the same number, the fraction will be equivalent to 5 fifths. They are also equivalent to 1 whole.
14	B	$20 \div 5 = 4$ and $24 \div 6 = 4$. So, this problem, when solved, would read 4 = 4.
15 PART A	600	When multiplying 10's, multiply the other digits and place the number of 0's in both factors after the answer. Each additional 0 represents another x 10.
15 PART B	9	When multiplying 10's, multiply the other digits and place the number of 0's in both factors after the answer. Each additional 0 represents another x 10.
15 PART C	30	When multiplying 10's, multiply the other digits and place the number of 0's in both factors after the answer. Each additional 0 represents another x 10.
16 PART A	4	You can multiply 2(Elm) x 4= 8 (cottonwood)
16 PART B	1	3-2=1. Simple subtraction gives the answer.

Question No.	Answer	Detailed Explanation
16 Part C	The number of cottonwood trees equals the number of oak and maple trees together.	5(oak) + 3 (maple) = 8 (cottonwood)
17	A, B	Since the problem reads "at least" it is acceptable to have more than one pair, but must have at least one pair of parallel sides. The triangle and circle do not have any parallel sides.
18	B	Only B has two of the four sections shaded, thus equivalent to $\frac{2}{4}$ or $\frac{1}{2}$.
19		 **Time spent reading** ▨ **5 hours** All six boxes should be shaded. 6x5=30
20 PART A	9	When completing division problems, think of the unknown factor and approach it like a multiplication problem. What number, when multiplied by the given factor, equals the product? All multiplication tables from 1-10 need to be memorized until they are automatic.
20 PART B	81	When completing division problems, think of the unknown factor and approach it like a multiplication problem. What number, when multiplied by the given factor, equals the product? All multiplication tables from 1-10 need to be memorized until they are automatic.

Question No.	Answer	Detailed Explanation
20 PART C	3	When completing division problems, think of the unknown factor and approach it like a multiplication problem. What number, when multiplied by the given factor, equals the product? All multiplication tables from 1-10 need to be memorized until they are automatic.
21 PART A	253 pounds	58+69+145=272 272-19=253
21 PART B	8 pounds	This is a multi step problem. First, solve to find out how many were picked the first four days (6 x 4 = 24). Then, determine how many were sold for each day (24÷3=8.)
22 PART A	8	When completing division problems, think of the unknown factor and approach it like a multiplication problem. What number, when multiplied by the given factor, equals the product? All multiplication tables from 1-10 need to be memorized until they are automatic.
22 PART B	30	When completing division problems, think of the unknown factor and approach it like a multiplication problem. What number, when multiplied by the given factor, equals the product? All multiplication tables from 1-10 need to be memorized until they are automatic.
22 PART C	8	When completing division problems, think of the unknown factor and approach it like a multiplication problem. What number, when multiplied by the given factor, equals the product? All multiplication tables from 1-10 need to be memorized until they are automatic.
22 PART D	6	When completing division problems, think of the unknown factor and approach it like a multiplication problem. What number, when multiplied by the given factor, equals the product? All multiplication tables from 1-10 need to be memorized until they are automatic.
22 PART E	5	When completing division problems, think of the unknown factor and approach it like a multiplication problem. What number, when multiplied by the given factor, equals the product? All multiplication tables from 1-10 need to be memorized until they are automatic.
23	A, C, D	Each question asks how much of the picture meets the qualifications based on the picture as a whole. We must also note that $\frac{1}{3} = \frac{2}{6}$.

Question No.	Answer	Detailed Explanation
24	772	When completing subtraction problems, vertically line up the digits by place value first. Then complete the subtraction process.
25 PART A	30	40-10=30 Round down if the digit under consideration is below 5. Otherwise, round up. When everything is a multiple of 10 it is much simpler to perform the operation.
25 PART B	120	140-20=120 Round down if the digit under consideration is below 5. Otherwise, round up. When everything is a multiple of 10 it is much simpler to perform the operation.
26 PART A	24	When completing division problems, think of the unknown factor and approach it like a multiplication problem. What number, when multiplied by the given factor, equals the product?
26 PART B	4 cartons	When completing division problems, think of the unknown factor and approach it like a multiplication problem. What number, when multiplied by the given factor, equals the product?
27		
28	11 cm	The sides are 3 + 4 + 8 + 11 + ? +15 =52 cm. Subtract to find the answer. 52- (the known sides)= unknown side. 52-41=11.
29	32 square inches	Multiply the length by the width to find the answer. 8 x 4 = 32 square inches
30 PART A	28	Approach each of these as "factor x factor = product". Consider which part of the equation is missing and use what you are given as hints.
30 PART B	6	Approach each of these as "factor x factor = product". Consider which part of the equation is missing and use what you are given as hints.

LumosLearning.com

Question No.	Answer	Detailed Explanation
30 PART C	7	Approach each of these as "factor x factor = product". Consider which part of the equation is missing and use what you are given as hints.
30 PART D	64	Approach each of these as "factor x factor = product". Consider which part of the equation is missing and use what you are given as hints.
31	32 feet	Perimeter asks you to determine the distance around the building. Squares have all sides of equal length. 4 x 8 = 32
32	B, D, E	Pictures B, D and E have six groups of seven objects.
33		$\frac{8}{8}$ is the same as 1. As long as the numerator and denominator are the same number, the fraction is equivalent to 1.
34 PART A	$2\frac{1}{3}$ times	At this point one can compare 3 blocks colored to 7 blocks. Each one represents $\frac{1}{3}$ of the white cat population. There are $\frac{3}{3}$ white cats and $\frac{7}{3}$ yellow cats. 3 goes into 7 $2\frac{1}{3}$ times.
34 PART B	4	This is a subtraction problem.
34 PART C	40 cats	Add all of the totals together to find this answer. 12+14+8+6=40
35	54 trees	6 x 9 = 54 Memorize the multiplication table up to ten.
36	29 grams	36 - 7 = 29 grams
37	72 people	9 x 8 = 72 This is another multiplication fact to memorize. 9 groups of 8 is equivalent to 72.

Question No.	Answer	Detailed Explanation
38		Recognize that $\dfrac{8}{6} = \dfrac{4}{3}$. Divide the top and bottom number of the first fraction by 2.
39 PART A	true	A rhombus has parallel sides.
39 PART B	true	A square has four equal sides and is therefore also a rhombus, though not all rhombuses are squares, because rhombuses might not always have right angles.

LumosLearning.com

Notes

End-Of-Year Assessment (EOY) - 2

Student Name: Start Time:

Test Date: End Time:

> **Here are some reminders for when you are taking the Grade 3 Mathematics End-Of-Year Assessment (EOY).**
>
> To answer the questions on the test, use the directions given in the question. If you do not know the answer to a question, skip it and go on to the next question. If time permits, you may return to questions in this session only. Do your best to answer every question.

1. 60 flowers were planted in 6 flower beds. The same number of flowers were planted in each bed. How many plants were planted in each flower bed? Write your answer in the box below.

2. Complete the bar graph to represent the number of first place ribbons awarded to Smallville H.S. in 2013. In 2013 the school received 20 first place ribbons.

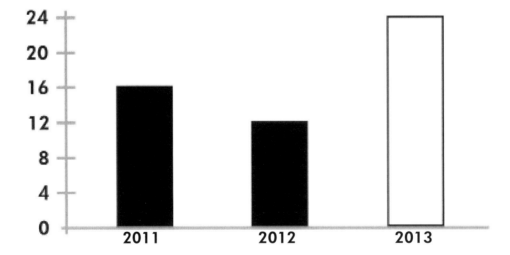

3. The graph below shows the number of each type of book in Jenny's home library. Complete the following exercises based on this information.

Books

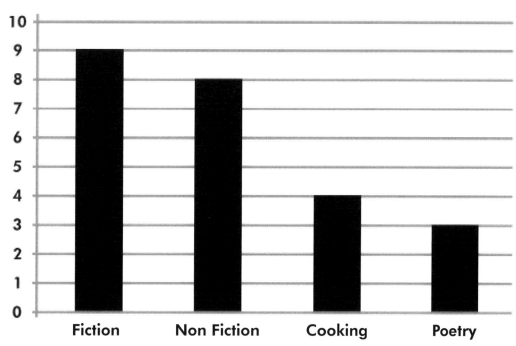

 Type

PART A

There are _____ times the number of fiction books as there are poetry books. Write your answer in the box below.

```
┌─────────────────────────────────────────┐
│                                         │
│                                         │
└─────────────────────────────────────────┘
```

PART B

How many more cooking books are there than poetry books? Write your answer in the box below.

```
┌─────────────────────────────────────────┐
│                                         │
│                                         │
└─────────────────────────────────────────┘
```

PART C

The number of non-fiction books is _____ more than the number of poetry books. Write your answer in the box below.

```

```

4. The graph below shows the number of each type of bike found on a school bike rack. Complete the following exercises based on this information.

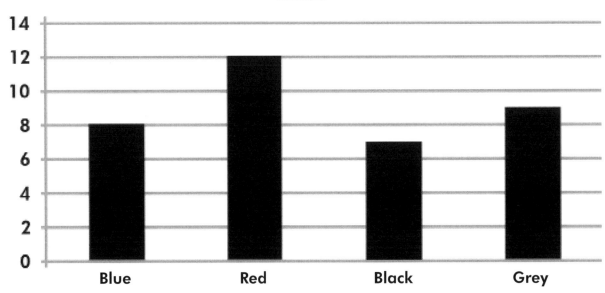

Bikes

■ Bikes

PART A

The number of red bikes is almost twice the number of _____ bikes. Write your answer in the box below.

```

```

PART B

How many fewer blue bikes are there than grey bikes? Write your answer in the box below.

```

```

       LumosLearning.com   ▶

PART C

What is the total number of bikes represented? Write your answer in the box below.

5. What is the length of this needle, in inches? Fill in the bubble corresponding to your answer choice.

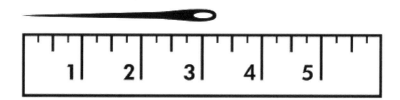

Ⓐ $3\frac{1}{4}$ inches

Ⓑ 3 inches
Ⓒ 2 inches

Ⓓ $2\frac{1}{4}$ inches

6. Solve the following equation. 6 x 7 =_____. Write your answer in the box below.

7. Solve the following.

PART A

25 candles are placed upon 5 tables. How many candles are there per table if divided evenly? Write your answer in the box below.

PART B

16 frogs are placed in 4 mud puddles. How many frogs are there per mud puddle if divided evenly? Write your answer in the box below.

PART C

36 cars are parked in 6 garages, evenly divided. How many cars are there in each garage? Write your answer in the box below.

PART D

What do each of the above word problems have in common? Explain your answer and write your explanation in the box below.

8. Supply the missing factor, product or quotient for each equation.

    $5 \times 6 = \boxed{}$

    $9 \times \boxed{} = 63$

    $54 \div 6 = \boxed{}$

    $5 \times 4 = \boxed{}$

9. Mrs. Brown had a birthday and wanted to give each student in her classroom a sack with 8 pieces of candy. She determined she would need to purchase 72 pieces of candy for this to be possible. Which of the following equations would determine the number of students in her class?

Ⓐ 72 - 8 = _____
Ⓑ 72 x 8 = _____
Ⓒ 72 ÷ 8 = _____
Ⓓ 72 + 8 = _____

10. There are 7 rows of 8 balls on the toy store shelves. How many balls are there in the toy store? Write your answer in the box below.

```



```

11. Which two of the following represent the equation 8 x 5?

Ⓐ five groups of eight horses
Ⓑ five cows and eight pigs
Ⓒ eight groups of dogs, five per group
Ⓓ eight pieces of paper, five get thrown in the trash
Ⓔ five bears chasing eight fish in a stream

12. A restaurant is serving meals to nine tables of six people.

PART A

How many people are in the party? Write your answer in the box below.

```



```

PART B

If one table finishes early and leaves. How many people remain? Write your answer in the box below.

```



```

13. 60 planes leave a certain airport every hour. How many planes are leaving the airport every 10 minutes if their take-offs are evenly spaced? Write your answer in the box below.

14. Mark the three of the following quadrilaterals that belong to the category of "rhombus".

Ⓐ

Ⓑ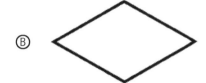

Ⓒ

Ⓓ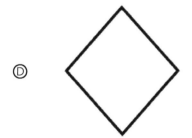

15. Divide the circle into four equal sections. Shade $\frac{1}{4}$

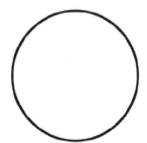

16. In the following rectangle, the perimeter is 30 cm.

10

What are the missing side dimensions? _____, _____ and _____ cm.

Write your answers in the box below.

17. A carpenter is measuring a room for trim around the perimeter.

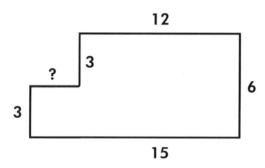

What is the missing side length if the perimeter is 42 feet? Write your answers in the box below.

18. Which answer equals "524 + 304" in expanded form?

Ⓐ 800+20+8
Ⓑ 800+20+6
Ⓒ 800+200+80
Ⓓ 8,000+800+60

19. **Supply the missing number.**

9 x 9 = ▢

▢ x 8 = 24

20. **Brent mowed lawns each morning last summer. Each morning for 7 mornings he moved 3 lawns. How many lawns did he mow in 7 days? Write your answer in the box below.**

21. **Chris bought 39 items at a yard sale for $9.75 each.**

PART A

About how much did he spend in all? Write your answer in the box below.

PART B

If Chris was able to resell 9 of the items for $21 each, about how much did he receive? Write your answer in the box below.

22. **Betty needed a quick estimate of how many muffins she had baked one morning in her bakery. The recipe said it makes approximately 18. She baked 11 batches. Which one of the following shows an expression to get the best estimate?**

Ⓐ 20 x 15
Ⓑ 20 x 20
Ⓒ 20 x 10
Ⓓ 18 x 10

LumosLearning.com   ▶

23. The following measuring cups have these amounts of liquid: $\dfrac{6}{8}$ and $\dfrac{3}{4}$ cups. Which statement below is true?

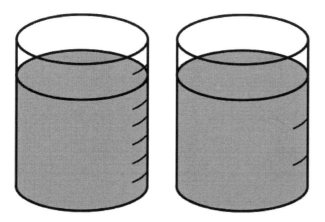

Ⓐ Cup A has less liquid than Cup B
Ⓑ Cup B has less liquid than Cup A
Ⓒ Both cups have the same amount of liquid.

24. Plot an equivalent fraction on the second number line.

The first fraction is $\dfrac{1}{3}$.

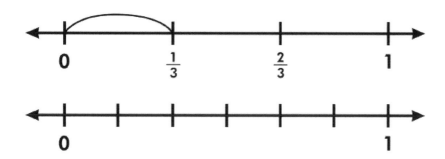

25. Supply the numerator in the second fraction, so that the fractions are equivalent. Write your answers in the box below.

$\dfrac{3}{6}$ and $\dfrac{?}{8}$

26. **Which one of the following fractions is not equivalent to 1?**

Ⓐ $\frac{6}{6}$

Ⓑ $\frac{3}{3}$

Ⓒ $\frac{12}{6}$

Ⓓ $\frac{8}{8}$

27. **Which two of the following fractions make this comparison true?**

$$\frac{10}{5} = \underline{\qquad}$$

Ⓐ 10

Ⓑ $\frac{12}{6}$

Ⓒ $\frac{5}{2}$

Ⓓ $\frac{8}{4}$

Ⓔ 5

28. **Plot the following points on the number line:** $\frac{7}{3}$ **and** $\frac{10}{4}$

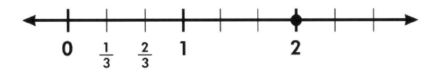

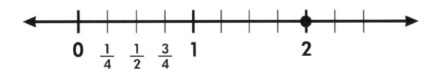

Which fraction is closer to 2? Write your answer in the box below.

29. Place the missing number in the box.

100 x 10 = ⬚

70 x ⬚ = 490

30. On the graph below, shade in the squares to indicate 28 gallons of water used. Each section equals 2 gallons.

Water

⬚ 2 gallons used

31. Which picture displays $\frac{1}{8}$? Fill in the bubble corresponding to your answer choice.

Ⓐ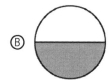

Ⓑ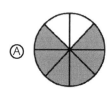

Ⓒ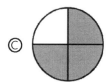

Ⓓ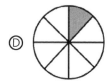

32. Which one of the following diagrams represents the fraction $\frac{4}{6}$? _____

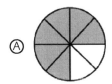 Ⓐ

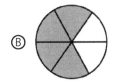 Ⓑ

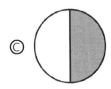 Ⓒ

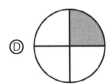 Ⓓ

33. Plot the following points on the number line: $\frac{7}{8}$ and $\frac{6}{5}$

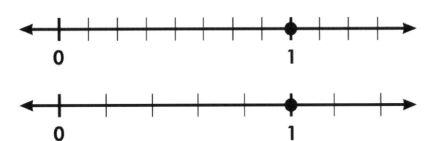

Which fraction is closer to 1? Write your answers in the box below.

LumosLearning.com

34. Below you will find a picture of a clock. Use the clock to answer the following questions.

PART A

What time is indicated on this clock?

Ⓐ Three thirty
Ⓑ Two thirty
Ⓒ Ten after six

PART B

What time will it be in 30 minutes? Write your answer in the box below.

```
┌─────────────────────────────────────────────┐
│                                             │
│                                             │
└─────────────────────────────────────────────┘
```

35. The clock show the time that Joe runs after school.

PART A

If he finishes 15 minutes later, what time will it be then?

Ⓐ 3:15 P.M.
Ⓑ 4:45 P.M.
Ⓒ 4:30 P.M.
Ⓓ 4:00 P.M.

PART B

Joe's coach rewards the team if they run an extra 15 minutes two days a week. What time would Joe stop running if he starts at the usual time and runs an extra 15 minutes? Write your answer in the box below.

36.   This cube contains 8 cubic cm of a liquid.

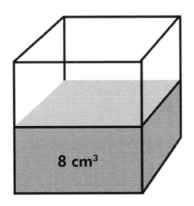

8 cm³

PART A

How many cubic cm would it have if the amount doubled? Write your answer in the box below.

PART B

Marty spilled 4 cubic cm worth of liquid from the larger container. How much is left in the cube? Write your answer in the box below.

37.   Fill in the missing number.

4 x _____ = 36

38. Here is a 6 inch by 8 inch rectangle.

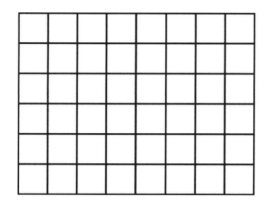

= 1 sq. inch

Determine the area. How many square inches does this rectangle contain? Write your answer in the box below.

39. Shade a 3 inch by 4 inch portion in the lower left corner of the rectangle.

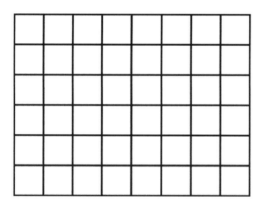

= 1 sq. inch

End of End-Of-Year Assessment (EOY) - 2

End-Of-Year Assessment (EOY) - 2

Answer Key

Question No.	Answer	Related Lumos Online Workbook	CCSS
1	10	Applying Multiplication & Division	3.OA.3
2	*	Graphs	3.MD.3
3 PART A	3	Graphs	3.MD.3
3 PART B	1	Graphs	3.MD.3
3 PART C	5	Graphs	3.MD.3
4 PART A	black	Graphs	3.MD.3
4 PART B	1	Graphs	3.MD.3
4 PART C	36 bikes	Graphs	3.MD.3
5	A	Measuring Length	3.MD.4
6 PART A	42	Understanding Multiplication	3.OA.1
7 PART A	5 candles	Understanding Division	3.OA.2
7 PART B	4 frogs	Understanding Division	3.OA.2
7 PART C	6 cars	Understanding Division	3.OA.2
7 PART D	*	Understanding Division	3.OA.2
8 PART A	30	Finding Unknown Values	3.OA.4
8 PART B	7	Finding Unknown Values	3.OA.4
8 PART C	9	Finding Unknown Values	3.OA.4
8 PART D	20	Finding Unknown Values	3.OA.4
9	C	Relating Multiplication & Division	3.OA.6
10	56 balls	Applying Multiplication & Division; Understanding Division; Understanding Multiplication	3.OA.3-1
11	A and C	Applying Multiplication & Division; Understanding Division; Understanding Multiplication	3.OA.3-2
12 PART A	54 people	Applying Multiplication & Division	3.OA.3-3
12 PART B	48 people	Applying Multiplication & Division	3.OA.3-3
13	6 planes	Applying Multiplication & Division; Finding Unknown Values	3.OA.3-4

      ▶

Question No.	Answer	Related Lumos Online Workbook	CCSS
14	B, C, and D	2-Dimensional Shapes	3.G.1
15	*	Shape Partitions	3.G.2
16	10, 5 and 5 cm	Perimeter	3.MD.8
17	3 feet	Perimeter	3.MD.8
18	A	Addition & Subtraction	3.NBT.2
19 PART A	81	Multiplication & Division Facts	3.OA.7
19 PART B	3	Multiplication & Division Facts	3.OA.7
20	21 lawns	Two-Step Problems; Multiplication & Division Facts; Relating Multiplication & Division; Multiplication & Division Properties; Finding Unknown Values; Applyingn Multiplication & Division; Understanding Division; Understanding Multiplication	3.OA.8-1
21 PART A	about $400	Rounding	3.NBT.1
21 PART B	about $200	Rounding	3.NBT.1
22	D	Rounding	3.NBT.1
23	C	Comparing Fractions	3.NF.3a-1
24	*	Comparing Fractions; Equivalent Fractions	3.NF.3a-2
25	4	Comparing Fractions; Equivalent Fractions	3.NF.3b-1
26	C	Equivalent Fractions	3.NF-3c
27	B and D	Equivalent Fractions	3.NF-3d
28	*	Fractions on the Number Line	3.NF.2
29 PART A	1,000	Multiplying Multiples of 10	3.NBT.3
29 PART B	7	Multiplying Multiples of 10	3.NBT.3
30	*	Graphs	3.MD.3
31	D	Fractions of a Whole	3.NF.1
32	B	Fractions of a Whole	3.NF.1
33	*	Fractions on the Number Line	3.NF.2
34 PART A	B	Telling Time; Elapsed Time	3.MD.1-1
34 PART B	3:00	Telling Time; Elapsed Time	3.MD.1-1
35 PART A	C	Telling Time; Elapsed Time; Liquid Volume & Mass	3.MD.1-2

Question No.	Answer	Related Lumos Online Workbook	CCSS
35 PART B	4:45 P.M.	Telling Time; Elapsed Time; Liquid Volume & Mass	3.MD.1-2
36 PART A	16	Liquid Volume & Mass	3.MD.2-2
36 PART B	12 cu. cm.	Liquid Volume & Mass	3.MD.2-2
37	9	Finding Unknown Values	3.OA.4
38	48 square inches	Area	3.MD.5
39	*	Area	3.MD.5

* See detailed explanation

LumosLearning.com

▶

End-Of-Year Assessment (EOY) - 2

Detailed Explanations

Question No.	Answer	Detailed Explanation
1	10	$60 \div 6 = 10$. Approach division problems like a multiplication problem with one factor missing. Think "What number times 6 equals 60?"
2	To add to the data from 2011 and 2012, we now have 2013 completed. The bars are shaded to reflect 20 ribbons in 2013. Each portion of the bar is equivalent to 4 ribbons.	
3 PART A	3	Poetry (3 books) x _____ = Fiction (9) The answer is 3.
3 PART B	1	Each line is worth 1 book. Cooking is one mark higher than Poetry.
3 PART C	5	The number of non-fiction books is 5 more than the number of poetry books. Poetry reaches the 3rd line. Non-fiction reaches to line number 8. $8-3=5$
4 PART A	black	(12 red) $\div$ 2 = 6 $(2 \times 6 = 12)$ The closest to 6 are the black bikes at 7.
4 PART B	1	9(grey) - 8(blue) = 1
4 PART C	36 bikes	$8 + 12 + 7 + 9 = 36$
5	A	The needle extends one mark past 3 inches. Each mark is equivalent to $\frac{1}{4}$ inch.
6 PART A	42	This is a multiplication fact that must be memorized for fluency. Think of this as 6 groups of 7.
7 PART A	5 candles	$25 \div 5 = 5$ 5 groups of 5 = 25.
7 PART B	4 frogs	4 groups of 4 = 16
7 PART C	6 cars	$36 \div 6 = 6$ 6 groups of 6 = 36

Question No.	Answer	Detailed Explanation
7 PART D		All three problems require of use division operation to answer the question. Ex 36 cars parked evenly in 6 garages is 36/6.
8 PART A	30	Approach a division problem as a multiplication problem. Think "what two factors when multiplied are equivalent to the given quotient?"
8 PART B	7	Approach a division problem as a multiplication problem. Think "what two factors when multiplied are equivalent to the given quotient?"
8 PART C	9	Approach a division problem as a multiplication problem. Think "what two factors when multiplied are equivalent to the given quotient?"
8 PART D	20	Approach a division problem as a multiplication problem. Think "what two factors when multiplied are equivalent to the given quotient?"
9	C	$8 \times 9 = 72$ 9 students each receive 8 pieces of candy
10	56 balls	$7 \times 8 = 56$
11	A and C	Only A and C show 8 groups of 5 or 5 groups of 8. $5 \times 8 = 40$. The other options are addition or subtraction instead.
12 PART A	54 people	$9 \times 6 = 54$. Nine groups of six is equivalent to 54. This is a multiplication fact that must be memorized.
12 PART B	48 people	We know that there are 54 people to begin. One table leaves. There are six sitting at each table. $54 - 6 = 48$.
13	6 planes	We start with 60 planes. A ten minute sample is taken. By dividing 60 by 10 the result is 6. Each 10 minute group of planes represents 6 planes.
14	B, C, and D	B - Because there are four equal sides, this is a rhombus. C - This square has four equal sides so it is a rhombus. D - There are four equal sides so it is a rhombus.
15		The circle requires two perpendicular lines to pass through the center of the circle. One section is shaded.

LumosLearning.com

Question No.	Answer	Detailed Explanation
16	10, 5 and 5 cm	The missing dimensions can be found by first determining the opposite side is 10 since this rectangle and opposite sides are equal. From that point, subtract the two known sides from 30. 30-20=10. Again, both sides are equal so divide ten in half. 10÷2=5. The result is sides of 5 cm.
17	3 feet	All dimensions are provided in the figure above, except for one. To find that dimension, add the dimensions known and subtract from the total. 3+3+12+6+15=39. 42-39= 3 feet.
18	A	We have 828 when the two numbers are added. For expanded form, the hundreds, tens, and ones places have to be displayed individually.
19 PART A	81	
19 PART B	3	
20	21 lawns	3 x 7 = 21. This is a common math fact to be memorized.
21 PART A	about $400	Round to 40 x $10. Chris spent about $400 in all. When an exact number is not required, estimating is a way to quickly find a close value.
21 PART B	about $200	Round to 10 x $20. Chris received about $200 in total.
22	D	Since the second number can be rounded to 10, we can use the first number as is. 18 x 10= 180. When multiplying by 10, just place a 0 after the number. 18 becomes 180.
23	C	 The picture shows the liquid level at the same height in these equal size containers. Also, we can multiply the $\frac{3}{4}$ x $\frac{2}{2}$ to arrive at a common denominator of 8. Once we multiply we have the same fraction of $\frac{6}{8}$.

Question No.	Answer	Detailed Explanation
24		Place a mark on the second number line the same distance from 0 as on the first number line. By reading the numbers we can see that the mark is placed at $\frac{2}{6}$. $\frac{2}{6}$ is $\frac{1}{3}$ x $\frac{2}{2}$.
25	4	In the first fraction, the numerator, 3, is half as much as the denominator. So, for the second fraction we again need a numerator half as much as the denominator. The denominator is 8 so the numerator must be 4.
26	C	This one is equivalent to 2 rather than 1. The numerator is twice as much as the denominator so the fraction is equivalent to 2.
27	B and D	The correct answers are those where the numerator is twice the denominator.
28		When these two points are marked on the number line, it is clear that $\frac{7}{3}$ is just slightly closer to 2 than the other fraction.
29 PART A	1,000	When multiplying by a 10, just multiply the beginning digits and place a zero after the number.
29 PART B	7	When multiplying by a 10, just multiply the beginning digits and place a zero after the number.

LumosLearning.com   ▶

Question No.	Answer	Detailed Explanation
30		**Water** ☐ **2 gallons used** 14 squares will need to be shaded so that the 28 gallons are represented. $28 \div 2 = 14$.
31	D	Only picture D has 8 sections with only one shaded. The others have either too much shading or an incorrect number of sections.
32	B	Only picture B has 6 sections with exactly 4 shaded. The others have either incorrect shading or an incorrect number of sections.
33		 When these two points are marked on the number line, it is clear that $\frac{7}{8}$ is just slightly closer to 1 than the other fraction.
34 PART A	B	The short hand indicates hours and the long hand indicates minutes.
34 PART B	3:00	30 minutes + 30 minutes = 60 minutes. We were 30 minutes past the hour, adding 30 more minutes brings us to the next hour.
35 PART A	C	Joe started running at 4:15 P.M. 15 + 15 = 30. It will be 4:30 P.M. when he finishes.
35 PART B	4:45 P.M.	4:30 + 15 more minutes is 4:45 P.M.

Question No.	Answer	Detailed Explanation
36 PART A	16	8 cubic cm x 2= 16 cubic cm The units stay the same. The operation is multiplication, 8 x 2= 16.
36 PART B	12 cu. cm.	If Marty started with 16 cu. cm. and 4 cu. cm. spilled then there are 12 remaining. 16-4=12. The units don't change.
37	9	Four groups of nine is 36. This is a basic multiplication fact to be memorized.
38	48 square inches	To figure area in square inches, multiply the two side dimensions. 6 x 8 = 48.
39		 On the picture we see that the number of squares shaded is four going across and three going up.

LumosLearning.com   ▶

Notes

Notes

     LumosLearning.com

Notes

Lumos StepUp™ is an educational App that helps students learn and master grade-level skills in Math and English Language Arts.

The list of features includes:

- Learn Anywhere, Anytime!

- Grades 3-8 Mathematics and English Language Arts

- Get instant access to the Common Core State Standards

- One full-length sample practice test in all Grades and Subjects

- Full-length Practice Tests, Partial Tests and Standards-based Tests

- 2 Test Modes: Normal mode and Learning mode

- Learning Mode gives the user a step-by-step explanation if the answer is wrong

- Access to Online Workbooks

- Provides ability to directly scan QR Codes

- And it's completely FREE!

http://lumoslearning.com/a/stepup-app

lumoslearning

About Online Workbooks

- When you buy this book, 1 year access to online workbooks included

- Access them anytime from a computer with an internet connection

- Adheres to the New Common Core State Standards

- Includes progress reports

- Instant feedback and self-paced

- Ability to review incorrect answers

- Parents and Teachers can assist in student's learning by reviewing their areas of difficulty

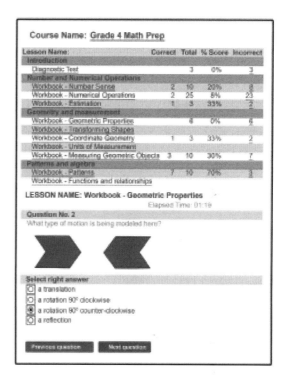

Report Name: Missed Questions

Student Name: Lisa Colbright
Cours Name: Grade 4 Math Prep
Lesson Name: Diagnostic Test

The faces on a number cube are labeled with the numbers 1 through 6. What is the probability of rolling a number greater than 4?

Answer Explanation

(C) On a standard number cube, there are six possible outcomes. Of those outcomes, 2 of them are greater than 4. Thus, the probability of rolling a number greater than 4 is "2 out of 6" or 2/6.

A)   1/6
B)   1/3
C) Correct Answer   2/6
D)   3/6

Made in the USA
San Bernardino, CA
18 February 2015